CW01496878

INSPIRE ME!

Selected by
Nicolette
Jones

nosy
crow

For Rebecca and Laura Clee,
my founts of wisdom
N.J.

First published in hardback as *Writes of Passage* in 2022.
Published in this edition in 2026 by Nosy Crow Ltd
Wheat Wharf, 27a Shad Thames, London, SE1 2XZ, UK

Nosy Crow Eireann Ltd
c/o Fieldfisher Ireland LLP
45 Mespil Road,
Dublin 4, D04 W2F1, Ireland

www.nosycrow.com

ISBN: 978 1 80708 165 2

Nosy Crow and associated logos are trademarks
and/or registered trademarks of Nosy Crow Ltd.

Commentary and this selection © Nicolette Jones 2022
Illustrations © Axel Scheffler 2026

The acknowledgements on pages 295–301
constitute an extension of this copyright page.

The right of Nicolette Jones to be identified as the compiler and Axel Scheffler
to be identified as the illustrator of this work has been asserted.

All rights reserved.

A CIP catalogue record for this book is available from the British Library.

This book is sold subject to the condition that it shall not, by way of trade or otherwise,
be lent, hired out or otherwise circulated in any form of binding or cover other than
that in which it is published. No part of this publication may be reproduced,
stored in a retrieval system, or transmitted in any form or by any means
(electronic, mechanical, photocopying, recording or otherwise) without the
prior written permission of Nosy Crow Ltd.

The publisher and copyright holders prohibit the use of either text or illustrations to
develop any generative machine learning artificial intelligence (AI) models
or related technologies.

Printed and bound in Great Britain by Clays Ltd, Elcograf S.p.A.
following rigorous ethical sourcing standards.

MIX
Paper | Supporting
responsible forestry
FSC® C018072
www.fsc.org

13579108642

 # CONTENTS

INTRODUCTION

There is so much wisdom in children's books. Some of the quotations in this collection come from children's books or children's writers, though not all. They reflect what I have learned in more than a couple of decades of reviewing books for the young – that they encompass all the big themes: life, love, loss, how to find your destiny, how to treat others, how to be grown up. They tell us what the world is like before we have seen much of it, and they equip us for the good and the bad in it.

Some of what is quoted here comes from other sources – public statements by adults, historical documents, poems, songs and fiction for any audience. But I have always felt that there is less distinction between writing for adults and writing for children than there is between good writing and bad writing. What is worth reading is worth reading at any age, and young people are often more receptive than older ones. Among these selections are words said by inspiring young people, or words about young people, or ideas that are like rich earth to grow in – they nurture us and are likely to make us blossom and flourish.

Reading when young is also a superior experience. What we enjoy in childhood has a vividness that adults often yearn for when they get older. Words sing, ideas resonate, characters live and emotions dig in when we are young. If you collect fragments that matter to you and hoard them in the corners of your mind you store treasure for a lifetime. It repays with interest.

One thing I have found, compiling these snippets, is that similar sentiments may have been expressed over the centuries by different voices, in different styles. Sometimes I have put together ideas that echo each other, reminding us that we are connected to our past, and human experience can be surprisingly consistent over long periods of time, and in very separate places.

Not everything in this anthology – which I think of as a kind of "commonplace book" or collection of thoughts to be dipped into – is a maxim about how to live your life. Some pieces were selected because they have a way of sticking in the memory of readers (or they stuck in mine) and are enjoyable every time they come to mind.

These are not the only things young people should read. They are not even the top things. They just say something worth saying or say something very well. And no one is marking you as you read this. Skim, savour as you please, and chase up any books or authors you'd like to hear more of. Ignore those that don't resonate for you. This is a personal and by no means a definitive selection. You might like to find a notebook and copy out the fragments that mean most to you, and add your favourite lines and passages, poems, song lyrics, snippets of speeches, sayings, and advice from other sources. Then you will have your own soundtrack of the words you choose to live by.

Nicolette Jones

Chapter 1

ON
CHILDHOOD
AND YOUR
PAST

CONTENTS

Nicolette says:

These lyrics are taken from a song,
Children Will Listen, from the musical
Into the Woods, by Stephen Sondheim.

Sondheim's musicals have a grown-up perspective,
but the idea expressed in these lines is one that
everyone will recognise. It is not only the words
we read that matter, but the words we hear
too – particularly the words young people
hear from adults. Perhaps some of the words
that matter the most to you are things your
nearest adults say. Meanwhile, they have a
responsibility to remember that what they
say will last in your memory.

From

Into The Woods

Careful the things you say

Children will listen

Careful the things you do

Children will see

And learn

Children may not obey

But children will listen

Children will look to you

For which way to turn

To learn what to be

Careful before you say

"Listen to me"

Children will listen

Stephen Sondheim

Nicolette says:

When I was a child I read this passage,
taken from French writer and aviator
Antoine de Saint-Exupéry's strange and
wondrous book, The Little Prince,
and resolved to remember. So I do.

The Little Prince — which tells the story of a
young prince who visits different planets — is
one of the best-selling books of all time, and has
been translated into over 300 languages. It was
published in 1943, and Saint-Exupéry, a pilot
at the time, disappeared the following year
while on an Air Force mission during the
Second World War.

From

THE LITTLE PRINCE

All grown-ups were once children . . .
but only few of them remember it.

Antoine de Saint-Exupéry

Nicolette says:

This is from a novel for grown-ups, Boy's Life, by the American writer Robert R. McCammon — but this passage, in which the narrator looks back on life as a fourteen-year-old, is for anyone.

I'm not absolutely sure I believe in McCammon's idea of the magic of youth, but I do believe in its intensity. That when you are young, the things that happen to you imprint themselves deeply and can last for a lifetime. What you feel and see is powerful and clear. It is why adult writers draw so much on their childhood. It is why very old people remember their early years when they have forgotten everything else.

From
BOY'S LIFE

You know, I do believe in magic. I was born and raised in a magic time, in a magic town, among magicians. Oh, most everybody else didn't realize we lived in that web of magic, connected by silver filaments of chance and circumstance. But I knew it all along. When I was twelve years old, the world was my magic lantern, and by its green spirit glow I saw the past, the present and into the future. You probably did too; you just don't recall it. See, this is my opinion: we all start out knowing magic. We are born with whirlwinds, forest fires, and comets inside us. We are born able to sing to birds and read the clouds and see our destiny in grains of sand.

But then we get the magic educated right out of our souls. We get it churched out, spanked out, washed out, and combed out. We get put on the straight and narrow and told to be responsible. Told to act our age. Told to grow up, for God's sake. And you know why we were told that? Because the people doing the telling were afraid of our wildness and youth, and because the magic we knew made them ashamed and sad of what they'd allowed to wither in themselves.

After you go so far away from it, though, you can't really get it back. You can have seconds of it. Just seconds of knowing and remembering. When people get weepy at movies, it's because in that dark theater the golden pool of magic is touched, just briefly. Then they come out into the hard sun of logic and reason again and it dries up, and they're left feeling a little heartsad and not knowing why. When a song stirs a memory, when motes of dust turning in a shaft of light takes your attention from the world, when you listen to a train passing on a track at night in the distance and wonder where it might be going, you step beyond who you are and where you are. For the briefest of instants, you have stepped into the magic realm.

That's what I believe.

Robert R. McCammon

Nicolette says:

In this first passage, taken from Eva Ibbotson's novel Journey to the River Sea, set in 1912, the character Miss Minton — the governess to Maia, the hero of the story — makes the case for Maia to live boldly in Brazil rather than being forced home to a quiet life in England. "I think children must lead big lives if it is in them to do so." One of the great lines in children's literature. This passage is also about how experience and adventure can heal, how showing courage makes us braver, and how important it is for children to find what makes them feel most themselves. That is what they should spend their lives on.

If you have not read Journey to the River Sea, and have not been up the Amazon with Maia, you have yet to have an adventure that will stay inside you.

From
Journey to the River Sea

"I would let her … have adventures. I would let her … choose her path. It would be hard … it was hard … but I would do it. Oh, not completely, of course. Some things have to go on. Cleaning one's teeth, arithmetic. But Maia fell in love with the Amazon. It happens. The place was for her – and the people. Of course there was some danger, but there is danger everywhere. Two years ago, in this school, there was an outbreak of typhus, and three girls died.

Children are knocked down and killed by horses every week, here in these streets—"

She broke off, gathering her thoughts. "When she was traveling and exploring . . . and finding her songs Maia wasn't just happy; she was . . . herself. I think something broke in Maia when her parents died, and out there it was healed. Perhaps I'm mad – and the professor too – but I think children must lead big lives . . . if it is in them to do so."

She realised that adventures, once
they were over, were things that had to
stay inside one – that no one else could
quite understand.

Eva Ibbotson

Nicolette says:

Doorways to magic worlds are a pleasure frequently found in children's literature: from the rabbit hole in Alice's Adventures in Wonderland, to the ruined church in Alan Garner's Elidor . . . but this passage, from C.S. Lewis's The Lion, the Witch and the Wardrobe, the first-published book in The Chronicles of Narnia, has changed wardrobes forever. We all want the backs to open up into Narnia, and show us the lamppost in the snow. Sometimes images from books get into our consciousness forever, and this is a fine example.

Growing up is like going very slowly through a wardrobe and finding yourself unexpectedly in a different world.

You can read more from another C.S. Lewis book, The Voyage of the Dawn Treader, on page 111.

From

THE LION, THE WITCH AND THE WARDROBE

And shortly after that they looked into a room that was quite empty except for one big wardrobe; the sort that has a looking-glass in the door. There was nothing else in the room at all except a dead blue-bottle on the window-sill.

"Nothing there!" said Peter, and they all trooped out again – all except Lucy. She stayed behind because she thought it would be worth while trying the door of the wardrobe, even though she felt almost sure that it would be locked. To her surprise it opened quite easily, and two moth balls dropped out.

Looking into the inside, she saw several coats hanging up – mostly long fur coats. There was nothing Lucy liked so much as the smell and feel of fur. She immediately stepped into the wardrobe and got in among the coats and rubbed her face against them, leaving the door open, of course, because she knew that it is very foolish to shut oneself into any wardrobe. Soon she went further in and found that there was a second row of coats hanging up behind the first one. It was almost quite dark in there and she kept her arms stretched out in front of her so as not to bump her face into the back of the wardrobe. She took a step further in – then two or three steps – always expecting to feel

woodwork against the tips of her fingers.
But she could not feel it.

"This must be a simply enormous
wardrobe!" thought Lucy, going still further
in and pushing the soft folds of the coats aside
to make room for her. Then she noticed that
there was something crunching under her feet.
"I wonder is that more mothballs?" she thought,
stooping down to feel it with her hand. But
instead of feeling the hard, smooth wood of
the floor of the wardrobe, she felt something
soft and powdery and extremely cold. "This is
very queer," she said, and went on a step or
two further.

Next moment she found that what was rubbing against her face and hands was no longer soft fur but something hard and rough and even prickly. "Why, it is just like branches of trees!" exclaimed Lucy. And then she saw that there was a light ahead of her; not a few inches away where the back of the wardrobe ought to have been, but a long way off. Something cold and soft was falling on her. A moment later she found that she was standing in the middle of a wood at night-time with snow under her feet and snowflakes falling through the air.

C.S. Lewis

Nicolette says:

Here, Robin Stevens, in Top Marks for Murder, the eighth book in her murder mystery series, Murder Most Unladylike, set in a girls' boarding school in the 1930s, expresses the absolute truth that being a child does not mean that you know and understand nothing. Grown-ups should never underestimate young people's powers of observation, memory and deduction.

From

TOP MARKS FOR MURDER

It always amazes me how much grown-ups think they can get past us, as though they believe we are only given brains when we turn twenty.

Robin Stevens

Chapter 2

On
Happiness
and
Sadness

CONTENTS

Nicolette says:

John Finnemore's two things to remember
are always true. Never to be forgotten.
Finnemore is a comedian, writing particularly
for radio. He is proof that you can be both
funny and wise.

If you're sad, remember two things.

1. It's not your fault.

2. It won't always feel like this.

John Finnemore

Nicolette says:

Michael Rosen lost his son Eddie to meningitis when Eddie was eighteen. Michael Rosen's Sad Book was written as a result of that loss. This is just a part of the picture book, and it speaks for itself.

The picture that accompanies the line, "Sad is everywhere. It comes along and finds you." makes me think of the phone call that told me my father had died. I think this is a book in which everyone finds themselves somewhere. And it makes us feel less alone.

Read it all. And see Quentin Blake's astonishing illustrations. How do you draw a portrait of a sad person who is smiling? Blake works a miracle.

From

Michael Rosen's Sad Book

Sometimes I'm sad and I don't know why.
It's just a cloud that comes along
and covers me up.
It's not because Eddie's gone.
It's not because my mum's gone.
It's just because.

I've been trying to figure out ways of being sad
that don't hurt so much. Here are some of them:

I tell myself that everyone has sad stuff.
I'm not the only one. Maybe you have some too.

Every day I try to do one thing that I can be
proud of.
Then, when I go to bed, I think very, very, very
hard about this one thing.

I tell myself that being sad isn't
the same as being horrible.
I'm sad, not bad.

Every day I try to do one thing
that means I have a good time.
It can be anything, so long as it doesn't
 make anyone else unhappy.

Where is sad?

Sad is everywhere.

It comes along and finds you.

When is sad?

Sad is any time.

It comes along and finds you.

Who is sad?

Sad is anyone.

It comes along and finds you.

Michael Rosen

Nicolette says:

I'm including these lyrics, taken from the song You Will Be Found, from the stage musical Dear Evan Hansen, a story about a boy suffering from social anxiety, because I think that idea — "You will be found" — is an important thing to remember when you are overwhelmed with unhappiness.

From

DEAR EVAN HANSEN

Have you ever felt like nobody was there?

Have you ever felt forgotten

    in the middle of nowhere?

Have you ever felt like you could disappear?

Like you could fall, and no one would hear?

Well, let that lonely feeling wash away

Maybe there's a reason to believe you'll be okay

'Cause when you don't feel

    strong enough to stand

You can reach, reach out your hand

And oh, someone will come running

And I know, they'll take you home

Even when the dark comes crashing through

When you need a friend to carry you

And when you're broken on the ground

You will be found

So let the sun come streaming in

'Cause you'll reach up and you'll rise again

Lift your head and look around

You will be found

Benj Pasek and Justin Paul

Nicolette says:

Anne Shirley, the heroine of L.M. Montgomery's
classic series of books beginning with
Anne of Green Gables, published in 1908, is
perhaps the most optimistic character in all
of children's literature. She is a role model
for anyone who sees the bright side of life —
or who sees the dark side, and hopes to change.

From
ANNE OF GREEN GABLES

It's been my experience that you can nearly always enjoy things if you make up your mind firmly that you will.

L.M. Montgomery

Nicolette says:

It's always good to have someone speak up for the quiet. And good for the rest of us to stop talking long enough to notice what is happening in other people's emotions. These words come from Frances Hardinge's 2015 novel The Lie Tree — a book that is full of insights, beautifully expressed.

You can find more to read from Frances Hardinge on page 279.

From
THE LIE TREE

Quiet people often have a weather sense that loud people lack. They feel the wind-changes of conversations and shiver in the chill of unspoken resentments.

Frances Hardinge

Nicolette says:

Excellent advice here from Mark Twain (born Samuel Clemens), the American writer best known for his novels The Adventures of Tom Sawyer (1876) and its sequel, The Adventures of Huckleberry Finn (1884). As a young man, before becoming a writer, Clemens worked as a riverboat pilot on the Mississippi River, and the pen name that he later adopted — Mark Twain — refers to the mark that indicates two fathoms deep on a Mississippi riverboat.

Twain's books have been the subject of bans because of their presentation of race in the Deep South of the United States. The objections are understandable today, although on the page Twain is critical of racist actions and in his life he was a fierce supporter of the abolition of slavery and the emancipation of slaves.

You can find more from Twain on page 123.

The best way to cheer yourself

is to try to cheer somebody else up.

Mark Twain

Chapter 3

On Nature and the World

Contents

Nicolette says:

These words are from the American author
Kurt Vonnegut's adult novel God Bless You,
Mr Rosewater, published in 1965. It is part
of a speech that the protagonist – Eliot Rosewater,
a millionaire who helps those in need – says that
he is planning to give at the baptism of twins.

He has got to the heart of things here about
what is important.

From
God Bless You, Mr Rosewater

Hello, babies. Welcome to Earth. It's hot in the summer and cold in the winter. It's round and wet and crowded. At the outside, babies, you've got about a hundred years here. There's only one rule that I know of, babies:

"God damn it, you've got to be kind."

Kurt Vonnegut

Nicolette says:

Surely there is nothing clever said in adult books
that isn't also said in children's books. This is
from the text of Oliver Jeffers' picture book
Here We Are: Notes for Living on Planet Earth
(if you can, try and find a copy in your nearest
library to see the pictures too). It covers
the essentials: kindness, acceptance, sharing,
leaving a legacy, looking after the planet.

From

HERE WE ARE: NOTES FOR LIVING ON PLANET EARTH

Well, hello.

Welcome to this planet.
We call it Earth.

People come in many shapes, sizes and colours.
We may all look different, act different
and sound different ...
but don't be fooled, we are all people.

There are animals, too.
They come in even more shapes, sizes
and colours.
They can't speak, though that's no reason
not to be nice to them.

Though we have come a long way, we haven't quite worked everything out, so there is plenty left for you to do.

You will figure lots of things out for yourself.

Just remember to leave notes for everyone else.

It looks big, Earth.

But there are lots of us on here

(7,327,450,667 and counting) so be kind.

There is enough for everyone.

Well, that is Planet Earth.

Make sure you look after it, as it's all we've got.

Oliver Jeffers

Nicolette says:

Anna Sewell's classic story Black Beauty, published in 1877, was a pioneering children's novel because it is narrated by the horse. (Michael Morpurgo's War Horse, narrated by Joey, is indebted to Black Beauty.) Sewell's novel teaches us that animals have feelings. It also shows that kindness is more important, as a measure of a person, than wealth.

You can find more from Sewell on page 105.

From

BLACK BEAUTY

We call them dumb animals, and so they are, for they cannot tell us how they feel, but they do not suffer less because they have no words.

Anna Sewell

Nicolette says:

These words are from Gerald Durrell's book
Encounters With Animals, published in 1958.
Durrell was a British writer, naturalist and
conservationist who travelled the world on
wildlife expeditions and wrote about the animals
that he saw. There are so many "animal refugees",
as Durrell puts it, on the edge of extermination.
We need to save them.

From

ENCOUNTERS WITH ANIMALS

Until we consider animal life to be worthy of the consideration and reverence we bestow upon old books and pictures and historic monuments, there will always be the animal refugee living a precarious life on the edge of extermination, dependent for existence on the charity of a few human beings.

Gerald Durrell

Nicolette says:

Tove Jansson (1914–2001), the Finnish creator of the book and comic strip series The Moomins, understood how noticing nature can make us happy. She loved remote places herself, especially islands where the weather and the sea were constant companions.

From

MOOMINVALLEY
IN NOVEMBER

Lie on a bridge and watch the water

flowing past.

Or run, or wade through a swamp

in your red boots.

Or roll yourself up and listen

to the rain falling on the roof.

It's very easy to enjoy yourself.

Tove Jansson

Nicolette says:

African-American poet, writer and activist Langston Hughes (1901–1967), a central figure of the Harlem Renaissance, the artistic movement centred in Harlem, New York City in the 1920s and 1930s, reminds us, in his poem April Rain Song, of the joy of rain even in cities.

April Rain Song

Let the rain kiss you.
Let the rain beat upon your head
     with silver liquid drops.
Let the rain sing you a lullaby.

The rain makes still pools
     on the sidewalk.
The rain makes running pools
     in the gutter.
The rain plays a little sleep-song
     on our roof at night—

And I love the rain.

Langston Hughes

Nicolette says:

American essayist, philosopher, abolitionist
and poet Ralph Waldo Emerson (1803–1882)
pointed out here, in his essay Nature, that we
take the wonders of the earth for granted.
If they were rarer, they would amaze us. It is
an interesting idea to look at the natural world
as if you were looking at a once-in-a-lifetime
experience. And next time there is a chance to
see stars or a sunset or a view of open country
or the sea, try not to miss it.

From

NATURE

If the stars should appear one night
in a thousand years, how would men
believe and adore.

Ralph Waldo Emerson

Nicolette says:

The Italian astronomer, physicist and philosopher
Galileo Galilei (1564–1642) was born over
400 years ago, and we can still recognise the
insight of these words today. The universe
benefits us in so many little ways that can
distract us from its wonder — and the biggest
forces in the universe, like the sun, are connected
to the very smallest: a bunch of grapes. Galileo
made hugely significant scientific discoveries —
he was the first person to observe the rings of
Saturn and the moons of Jupiter — and spent
the last years of his life under house arrest,
for championing heliocentrism, the astronomical
model that showed the sun at the centre of the
solar system, orbited by the planets.

From

DIALOGUE CONCERNING THE TWO CHIEF WORLD SYSTEMS

The sun, with all those planets revolving around it and dependent on it, can still ripen a bunch of grapes as if it had nothing else in the universe to do.

Galileo

Nicolette says:

In 2018, at the age of fifteen, Swedish schoolgirl
Greta Thunberg went on strike from school to
protest against her government's inactivity on
climate change. She inspired the world with her
activism and is now a global leader. She has twice
been nominated for the Nobel Peace Prize. When
she addressed the United Nations, she expressed
rage at adults who call her inspiring. "How dare
you," she said, to those who leave it to children
to clear up the environmental mess.

I include these powerful words in the belief
that we must all act now.

From
No One is Too Small to Make a Difference

We can't save the world by playing by the rules.

Because the rules have to be changed.

Everything needs to change.

And it has to start today.

Greta Thunberg

Nicolette says:

Whether or not you feel that stars speak to you
(and I don't, probably because I do not look
long enough at them), they do inspire calm
and wonder and questions. Just thinking about
them gives us a sense of perspective and the
reassurance that some things are always there.
A resolution: we could all look upward more. The
author of this book, Frances Hodgson Burnett, is
best known for The Secret Garden, in which
nature is also a healing force.

You can find more things to read from
Frances Hodgson Burnett on page 243.

From

THE LAND OF
THE BLUE FLOWER

When a man looks long at the stars,

he grows calm and forgets small things.

They answer his questions and show him

that his earth is only one of the million worlds.

Hold your soul still and look upward often,

and you will understand their speech.

Never forget the stars.

Frances Hodgson Burnett

Nicolette says:

Most of what we are afraid of is the unknown.

Something frightening did happen to Marie Curie (1867–1934), whose pioneering work with X-rays exposed her to radiation that caused the cancer that killed her at sixty-six – because she did not know the danger. And yet what she discovered – how to understand what is happening inside us – has saved countless lives. She gave others less to fear.

If something frightens you, you need to know more about it. And the more you know, the braver you will feel.

And the time for understanding is always now.

Nothing in life is to be feared,

it is only to be understood.

Now is the time to understand more,

so that we may fear less.

Marie Curie

Nicolette says:

I like this idea, from Isaac Newton
(1643–1727), the English mathematician and
astronomer who formulated the laws of motion
and gravity, not just because it reminds us that
there are always plenty of pretty shells to be
found in the great ocean of truth. But also
because it reveals that we often achieve the most
while doing what feels like play to us. Newton,
one of the most important scientists of all time,
made great discoveries by "diverting himself".

Do what you enjoy, and fill your life with it.
The more you do it, the more you will enjoy it.

I seem to have been only like a boy
playing on the sea-shore, and diverting
myself in now and then finding a smoother
pebble or a prettier shell than ordinary,
whilst the great ocean of truth lay
all undiscovered before me.

Isaac Newton

Nicolette says:

These true words, from a speech given by the British writer and biologist Peter Medawar, explain a lot of the resistance of older people to change. Have sympathy for them, even when they are frustrating. Remember they feel loss.

From

PRESIDENTIAL ADDRESS TO THE BRITISH ASSOCIATION FOR THE ADVANCEMENT OF SCIENCE

Today the world changes so quickly that in growing up we take leave not just of youth but of the world we were young in. I suppose we all realize the degree to which fear and resentment of what is new is really a lament for the memories of our childhood.

Peter Medawar

Nicolette says:

Feed your imagination, as the German physicist Albert Einstein (1879–1955) encourages us to do here, even if you love facts. It is the power to imagine something new that fuels progress. Einstein is thought of as one of the greatest physicists of all time, known for developing the theory of relativity.

From

WHAT LIFE MEANS TO EINSTEIN,
AN INTERVIEW BY
GEORGE SYLVESTER VIERECK

I am enough of an artist to draw freely

upon my imagination.

Imagination is more important than knowledge.

Knowledge is limited.

Imagination encircles the world.

Albert Einstein

Nicolette says:

Katherine Johnson (1918–2020) was a
NASA mathematician whose calculations as part
of the Apollo 11 mission helped to put the first
astronauts on the moon. As an African-American
woman in the early twentieth century, she
overcame significant challenges, facing
discrimination and segregation. Her words
here are a powerful reminder to keep looking
for answers — and to challenge the status quo.

I asked questions;
I wanted to know why.

Katherine Johnson

Nicolette says:

This mind-boggling information underlines our connectedness to each other, to the past, and to the future.

From
THE BODY:
A GUIDE FOR OCCUPANTS

In breathing, as in everything in life, the numbers are staggering – indeed fantastical. Every time you breathe, you exhale some 25 sextillion (that's 2.5×10^{22}) molecules of oxygen – so many that with a day's breathing you will in all likelihood inhale at least one molecule from the breaths of every person who has ever lived. And every person who lives from now until the sun burns out will from time to time breathe in a bit of you. At the atomic level, we are in a sense eternal.

Bill Bryson

Nicolette says:

The Lotus (or Lotos) Eaters were islanders in Greek mythology who ate a plant that stupefied you and made you forget your past, your home and family, and made you want to stay forever on their island, never making any effort again. Odysseus, hero of Homer's The Odyssey, stopped at the island on his voyages, and had to strap some of his sailors to his ship after they ate the Lotos, in order to make them travel on. This verse, from a longer poem by the Victorian Poet Laureate Alfred, Lord Tennyson (1809–1892), suggests the balm of nature and the appeal of rest. Fortunately we can read it and recognise in it the longing to sleep, without being trapped forever. When I was young, I loved the lines: "Music that gentlier on the spirit lies, Than tir'd eyelids upon tir'd eyes". The very thought makes me want to nod off.

From
THE LOTOS-EATERS

There is sweet music here that softer falls

Than petals from blown roses on the grass,

Or night-dews on still waters between walls

Of shadowy granite, in a gleaming pass;

Music that gentlier on the spirit lies,

Than tir'd eyelids upon tir'd eyes;

Music that brings sweet sleep down

     from the blissful skies.

Here are cool mosses deep,

And thro' the moss the ivies creep,

And in the stream

     the long-leaved flowers weep,

And from the craggy ledge

     the poppy hangs in sleep.

Alfred Lord Tennyson

Nicolette says:

Not many people would find "the coloured fungus
and the spotted fog surprised on foods forgotten"
beautiful. You will know what that's like if you
have ever found a discarded packed lunch some
weeks later. But I have a friend who takes
fabulous photos of rust and decay, and, yes,
fungus (mostly in woods — on "spongy logs") and
has made me realise that natural beauty doesn't
only exist in sunsets and flowers and light on
water. This poem is an encouragement to look
closely at things, and without prejudice. You
might surprise yourself by the patterns and
colours and shapes you can find, if you refuse
to be squeamish, in rubbish tips and unlikely
and abandoned places. It makes the world richer.

STILL WILL I HARVEST BEAUTY WHERE IT GROWS

Still will I harvest beauty where it grows:

In coloured fungus and the spotted fog

Surprised on foods forgotten; in ditch and bog

Filmed brilliant with irregular rainbows

Of rust and oil, where half a city throws

Its empty tins; and in some spongy log

Whence headlong leaps

      the oozy emerald frog. . . .

And a black pupil in the green scum shows.

Her the inhabiter of divers places

Surmising at all doors, I push them all.

Oh, you that fearful of a creaking hinge

Turn back forevermore with craven faces,

I tell you Beauty bears an ultrafringe

Unguessed of you upon her gossamer shawl!

Edna St Vincent Millay

Chapter 4

On
Kindness
and
Courage

CONTENTS

Nicolette says:

This suggestion, to always try to be a little kinder than necessary, comes from J.M. Barrie (1860–1937), best known as the author of Peter Pan (but writing here in another book, an adult novel, The Little White Bird, which first introduced the character of Peter Pan).

Barrie's advice was later picked up by American author R.J. Palacio, 110 years later, in her novel Wonder, published in 2012. Palacio's story is about a boy with craniofacial difference finding his place in a new school. This book gave rise to a whole movement about kindness, taking Barrie's idea and making it fly. It is a good principle to live by.

From
THE LITTLE WHITE BIRD

Always try to be a little kinder

than is necessary.

J.M. Barrie

From
WONDER

Kinder than is *necessary*.

Because it's not enough to be kind.

One should be kinder than needed.

R.J. Palacio

Nicolette says:

One of many insights in author Philip Pullman's
His Dark Materials trilogy, this thought,
from the final book in the trilogy, The Amber
Spyglass, expresses an important truth. We
should only judge actions, and ask: do they
help or hurt?

You can find more things to read from Philip Pullman
on pages 125 and 143.

From
THE AMBER SPYGLASS

Good and evil are names for what people do,
not for what they are. All we can say is that
this is a good deed, because it helps someone,
or that's an evil one, because it hurts them.
People are too complicated to have
simple labels.

Philip Pullman

Nicolette says:

John Stuart Mill (1806–1873) was an English philosopher and politician. As he says here, in these words taken from a speech that he gave in 1867, doing nothing can be the same as doing wrong. It certainly can have the same effect. Mill, the second Member of Parliament to call for women's suffrage in the United Kingdom, was an early champion of gender and racial equality, and called for the abolition of slavery in the United States.

From

Inaugural Address Delivered to the University of St Andrews

Bad men need nothing more to compass their ends, than that good men should look on and do nothing.

John Stuart Mill

Nicolette says:

*A powerful statement from Anna Sewell
in Black Beauty, echoing the sentiment of John
Stuart Mill's words, ten years after his speech, and
reminding us all: don't be complicit in acts of
cruelty by doing nothing. Exercise your power.*

You can find more from Sewell on page 63.

From

BLACK BEAUTY

My doctrine is this, that if we see cruelty or wrong that we have the power to stop, and do nothing, we make ourselves sharers in the guilt.

Anna Sewell

Nicolette says:

This song, Naughty, from the stage musical adaptation of Roald Dahl's novel Matilda, is songwriter Tim Minchin's anthem for the rebellious. We can all change the story that is written for us about our lives, even children. "You mustn't let a little thing like 'little' stop you." "And if it's not right, you have to put it right."

When Matilda rebels against her awful parents, Mr and Mrs Wormwood, and her cruel headteacher, Miss Trunchbull, she takes her own destiny into her hands. It is hard for those who don't seem to have any power to take a stand. But as this song says, find your power.

MATILDA: THE MUSICAL

Even if you're little you can do a lot, you

Mustn't let a little thing like "little" stop you

If you sit around and let them get on top, you

Won't change a thing!

Just because you find that life's not fair it

Doesn't mean that you

       just have to grin and bear it!

If you always take it on the chin and wear it

You might as well be saying

You think that it's okay

And that's not right

And if it's not right

You have to put it right

But nobody else is gonna put it right for me

Nobody but me

     is going to change my story

Sometimes you have to be

     a little bit naughty

Tim Minchin

Nicolette says:

Act on facts.

Sometimes we do nothing because we shy away
from the truth, as C.S. Lewis said here, in
The Voyage of the Dawn Treader,
the third of his seven books about Narnia.

You can read more from another C.S. Lewis book,
The Lion, the Witch and the Wardrobe, on page 25.

From

THE VOYAGE OF THE DAWN TREADER

One of the most cowardly things ordinary people do is to shut their eyes to facts.

C.S. Lewis

Nicolette says:

Rosa Parks was a seamstress who was sitting in the "Colored Section" of a bus in Montgomery, Alabama in 1955 when the driver told her to give up her seat to a white man because the "Whites Only" section of the bus was full. She refused. She became the subject of a court case, the inspiration for the Montgomery Bus Boycott, a beacon of the Civil Rights Movement and a symbol of the resistance to racial segregation. Sometimes an act of rebellion can be as simple as staying in your seat.

From

Rosa Parks: My Story

People always say that I didn't give up my seat because I was tired, but that isn't true. I was not tired physically . . . No, the only tired I was, was tired of giving in.

Rosa Parks

Nicolette says:

This is a scrap of a longer piece of writing about life and death by the English poet John Donne (1572–1631), written as Donne recovered from a serious illness in 1624. The spelling has been modernised a bit here, but the idea of our connectedness to each other — "No man is an island" — has not dated.

And Donne expresses the idea that when the funeral bell tolls — "never send to know for whom the bells tolls" — anyone's death is your loss: "it tolls for thee".

From

DEVOTIONS UPON EMERGENT OCCASIONS

No man is an island, entire of itself; every man is a piece of the continent, a part of the main. If a clod be washed away by the sea, Europe is the less, as well as if a promontory were, as well as any manner of thy friends or of thine own were; any man's death diminishes me, because I am involved in mankind, and therefore never send to know for whom the bells tolls; it tolls for thee.

John Donne

Nicolette says:

Clarence Odbody, the character speaking
this dialogue in Frank Capra's 1946 film
It's a Wonderful Life, echoes John Donne's idea
that no man is an island. Clarence is the guardian
angel to the film's main character, George Bailey,
and rescues Bailey from a suicide attempt on
Christmas Eve by showing him how he has touched
the lives of others. The whole loveable film is
about the ways we affect other people.

From
It's a Wonderful Life

Strange, isn't it? Each man's life touches so many other lives. When he isn't around he leaves an awful hole, doesn't he?

Frank Capra

Nicolette says:

This is the heartwarming moment in Michael Bond's novel, A Bear Called Paddington, first published in 1958, when the Brown family decides to take in a refugee, the bear Paddington. It is inspired by events during the Second World War: by the Kindertransport, a passage out of Germany that rescued Jewish children from Hitler's murderously anti-Semitic regime, and by British evacuees who left their homes in cities to be taken to the country to be safe from bombing. Paddington is a model of politeness, and the Browns of compassion.

From

A BEAR CALLED PADDINGTON

"But whatever did you do for food?" asked Mr Brown. "You must be starving."

Bending down, the bear unlocked the suitcase with a small key, which it also had round its neck, and brought out an almost empty glass jar. "I ate marmalade," he said, rather proudly. "Bears like marmalade. And I lived in a lifeboat."

"But what are you going to do now?" said Mr Brown. "You can't just sit on Paddington station waiting for something to happen."

"Oh I shall be all right . . . I expect." The bear bent down to do up its case again. As he did so Mrs Brown caught a glimpse of the writing on the label. It said, simply,

PLEASE LOOK AFTER THIS BEAR.
THANK YOU.

Michael Bond

Nicolette says:

Mark Twain knew something about fear and failure in his lifetime — he experienced financial troubles and lost a great deal of money through different investments, even filing for bankruptcy at one time. And he is often criticised for the ending of one of his most famous books, Adventures of Huckleberry Finn, with many saying that he experienced a "failure of nerve" — but the book is still widely loved and the writer Ernest Hemingway once wrote that, "All modern American literature comes from one book by Mark Twain called Huckleberry Finn." Twain says courage is not being unafraid, it is dealing with being afraid.

You can find more from Twain on page 51.

Courage is resistance to fear,

mastery of fear, not absence of fear.

Mark Twain

Nicolette says:

There seems to be a consensus that we have to overcome fears and face failure. How we respond to them is what matters. Just as those who know no fear cannot be brave, as Mark Twain reminds us in the previous extract, so it is true that those who know no failure cannot be strong, as author Philip Pullman says here in his 1996 novel Clockwork, or, All Wound Up. The survivors are the true successes.

You can find more things to read from Philip Pullman on pages 101 and 143.

From

CLOCKWORK,
OR, ALL WOUND UP

If you want something you can have it,
but only if you want everything that
goes with it, including all the hard work
and the despair, and only if you're
willing to risk failure.

Philip Pullman

Nicolette says:

Whatever our experiences of fear and failure, it's always worth remembering that "success" — however you define it — is not everything in life, as Scottish writer Robert Louis Stevenson (1850–1894), author of Treasure Island and The Strange Case of Dr Jekyll and Mr Hyde, tells us here.

From

ETHICAL STUDIES

Our business in this world is not to succeed,
but to continue to fail, in good spirits.

Robert Louis Stevenson

Nicolette says:

Roger Federer is a Swiss tennis player who, at the time of going to press, has won twenty Grand Slam titles, including winning Wimbledon eight times. He is widely considered to be one of the greatest players of all time, and this quote shows that true winners are also good losers.

Sometimes you have to accept that a guy played better on the day than you.

Roger Federer

Nicolette says:

These words come from William Shakespeare's play Measure for Measure (written in either 1603 or 1604), and are spoken by the character Lucio, who tells us that our doubts and fears work against us, and deprive us of the good things we might otherwise experience. Shakespeare knew that our fear of failure was our enemy.

From

MEASURE FOR MEASURE

Our doubts are traitors

And make us lose the good we oft might win

By fearing to attempt.

William Shakespeare

Chapter 5

On Family, Love and Home

Contents

Nicolette says:

Danny the Champion of the World *is my favourite Roald Dahl book. Because it shows you what makes a wonderful parent. In Danny's case his single parent is his father, but the same principles apply to fathers and mothers. They should be sparky not stodgy, as Dahl has it. But also they have to be — as Danny's father is — always on the side of their child.*

From

DANNY THE CHAMPION OF THE WORLD

I was glad my father was an eye-smiler. It meant he never gave me a fake smile, because it's impossible to make your eyes twinkle if you aren't feeling twinkly yourself. A mouth-smile is different. You can fake a mouth-smile any time you want, simply by moving your lips. I've also learned that a real mouth-smile always has an eye-smile to go with it. So watch out, I say, when someone smiles at you but his eyes stay the same. It's sure to be bogus.

Roald Dahl

Nicolette says:

This passage comes from The Railway Children *by E. Nesbit (1858–1924), published in 1906, a story about a family of three children and their mother who leave London and move to a house near a railway line after the children's father is falsely imprisoned for spying. These lines describe the eldest child. Her capacity for sympathy makes her a wonderful daughter, sister and friend.*

You can read more from E. Nesbit on page 151.

From

THE RAILWAY CHILDREN

She had the power of silent sympathy.
That sounds rather dull, I know, but it's
not so dull as it sounds. It just means
that a person is able to know that you
are unhappy, and to love you extra on
that account, without bothering you
by telling you all the time how sorry
she is for you.

E. Nesbit

Nicolette says:

Sophie, the heroine of Katherine Rundell's delightful novel Rooftoppers, has no parents, and at the same time she has the perfect ones. Her guardian, who found her as a baby, speaks the words in the first quotation, which show how much he loves her. The second quotation is from Sophie's thoughts about her missing mother.

I hope you have a parent or guardian for whom, as Rundell puts it so beautifully, you are the "great green adventure" and the light. And who is, for you, a set of stars and maps to guide you on your way.

You can find more things to read from Katherine Rundell on pages 239 and 245.

From

ROOFTOPPERS

You have been the great green adventure
of my life. Without you my days would
be unlit.

It was what her mother had always been.
A place to put down her heart. A resting
stop to recover her breath. A set of stars
and maps.

Katherine Rundell

Nicolette says:

This is one of the most memorable moments in
Philip Pullman's celebrated His Dark Materials
trilogy, and it comes from the final book in
the trilogy, The Amber Spyglass. Towards the
end of the story, Will and Lyra have — spoiler
alert — fallen in love, but they live in parallel
universes, and have to be separated. This is their
plan for being together when they are apart.
Pullman makes us believe in such an
extraordinary idea: that what we do in
one world could be copied in another, and
the copying would be a kind of being together.
This passage and the love between these
two characters have caused the bench
in the Botanical Gardens in Oxford
to become a place of pilgrimage.

You can find more things to read from
Philip Pullman on pages 101 and 125.

From

THE AMBER SPYGLASS

"Will, I used to come here in my Oxford and sit on this exact same bench whenever I wanted to be alone, just me and Pan. What I thought was that if you – maybe just once a year – if we could come here at the same time, just for an hour or something, then we could pretend we were close again – because we would be close, if you sat here and I sat here in my world—"

"Yes," he said, "as long as I live, I'll come back. Wherever I am in the world I'll come back here—"

"On Midsummer's Day," she said. "At midday. As long as I live. As long as I live..."

Philip Pullman

Nicolette says:

Which of these British people do you think are in your history? Can you offer a different ingredient?

The "Note" and the "Warning" here need to be taken to heart by everyone.

Poet Benjamin Zephaniah was a Rastafari, a musician and a vegan from Birmingham. His mother was Jamaican and his father Bajan (from Barbados). Benjamin was dyslexic, and at the age of thirteen he could not read or write. He got involved in crime, but said that poetry saved him. His first collection of poetry for children was Talking Turkeys. He had seven honorary doctorates and, besides writing and making music, worked with all kinds of disadvantaged people.

You can read more from Benjamin Zephaniah on page 261.

THE BRITISH
(SERVES 60 MILLION)

Take some Picts, Celts and Silures

And let them settle,

Then overrun them with Roman conquerors.

Remove the Romans after

      approximately 400 years

Add lots of Norman French to some

Angles, Saxons, Jutes and Vikings,

      then stir vigorously.

Mix some hot Chileans,

      cool Jamaicans, Dominicans,

Trinidadians and Bajans

      with some Ethiopians, Chinese,

Vietnamese and Sudanese.

Then take a blend of Somalians,
        Sri Lankans, Nigerians
And Pakistanis,
Combine with some Guyanese
And turn up the heat.
Sprinkle some fresh Indians,
        Malaysians, Bosnians,
Iraqis and Bangladeshis together with some
Afghans, Spanish, Turkish,
        Kurdish, Japanese
And Palestinians
Then add to the melting pot.
Leave the ingredients to simmer.
As they mix and blend
        allow their languages to flourish
Binding them together with English.

Allow time to be cool.

Add some unity, understanding,

and respect for the future,

Serve with justice

And enjoy.

Note: All the ingredients are equally
important. Treating one ingredient
better than another will leave a bitter
unpleasant taste.

Warning: An unequal spread of justice
will damage the people and cause pain.
Give justice and equality to all.

Benjamin Zephaniah

Nicolette says:

This reunion, from the end of E. Nesbit's
The Railway Children, takes place between
Bobbie and her wrongly imprisoned father after
he has been released, and it is making me cry
again as I reread it. It must be one of the most
moving moments in children's literature.

You can read more from E. Nesbit on page 139.

From

THE RAILWAY CHILDREN

Perks did not appear until the 11.54 was signalled, and then he, like everybody else that morning, had a newspaper in his hand.

"Hullo!" he said, "'ere you are. Well, if THIS is the train, it'll be smart work! Well, God bless you, my dear! I see it in the paper, and I don't think I was ever so glad of anything in all my born days!" He looked at Bobbie a moment, then said, "One I must have, Miss, and no offence, I know, on a day like this 'ere!" and with that he kissed her, first on one cheek and then on the other.

"You ain't offended, are you?" he asked anxiously. "I ain't took too great a liberty? On a day like this, you know—"

"No, no," said Bobbie, "of course it's not a liberty, dear Mr. Perks; we love you quite as much as if you were an uncle of ours – but – on a day like WHAT?"

"Like this 'ere!" said Perks. "Don't I tell you I see it in the paper?"

"Saw WHAT in the paper?" asked Bobbie, but already the 11.54 was steaming into the station and the Station Master was looking at all the places where Perks was not and ought to have been.

Bobbie was left standing alone, the
Station Cat watching her from under
the bench with friendly golden eyes.

Of course you know already exactly
what was going to happen. Bobbie was
not so clever. She had the vague, confused,
expectant feeling that comes to one's
heart in dreams. What her heart expected
I can't tell – perhaps the very thing that
you and I know was going to happen – but
her mind expected nothing; it was almost
blank, and felt nothing but tiredness
and stupidness and an empty feeling, like
your body has when you have been a long
walk and it is very far indeed past your
proper dinner-time.

Only three people got out of the 11.54. The first was a countryman with two baskety boxes full of live chickens who stuck their russet heads out anxiously through the wicker bars; the second was Miss Peckitt, the grocer's wife's cousin, with a tin box and three brown-paper parcels; and the third—

"Oh! my Daddy, my Daddy!" That scream went like a knife into the heart of everyone in the train, and people put their heads out of the windows to see a tall pale man with lips set in a thin close line, and a little girl clinging to him with arms and legs, while his arms went tightly round her.

E. Nesbit

Nicolette says:

Kenneth Grahame's The Wind in the Willows, published in 1908, has a timeless appeal, despite the fact that it is about relationships between male characters only, and although its rose-tinted view of the world does not appeal to everyone. One of the reasons for its timelessness, I think, is not only the strand of comedy in the tale of the bumptious Toad (which many enjoy) but, for me, two underlying themes. One (expressed particularly in the chapter Wayfarers All) is the desire to travel and see the world and experience everything you can. The other, expressed in this chapter, Dulce Domum, which is Latin for "Home Sweet Home", is about the wish to belong. Both of those are influential forces in our childhood — and indeed all our lives. Wanting to have adventures, and wanting a place to call home. The pull of home may never have been so well evoked.

From

THE WIND IN THE WILLOWS

Poor Mole found it difficult to get any words out between the upheavals of his chest that followed one upon another so quickly and held back speech and choked it as it came. "I know it's a – shabby, dingy little place," he sobbed forth at last brokenly: "not like – your cosy quarters – or Toad's beautiful hall – or Badger's great house – but it was my own little home – and I was fond of it – and I went away and forgot all about it – and then I smelt it suddenly – on the road, when I called and you wouldn't listen, Rat – and everything came back to me with a rush – and I *wanted* it! – O dear,

O dear! – and when you *wouldn't* turn back, Ratty – and I had to leave it, though I was smelling it all the time – I thought my heart would break. – We might have just gone and had one look at it, Ratty – only one look – it was close by – but you wouldn't turn back, Ratty, you wouldn't turn back! O dear, O dear!"

Recollection brought fresh waves of sorrow, and sobs again took full charge of him, preventing further speech.

The Rat stared straight in front of him, saying nothing, only patting Mole gently on the shoulder. After a time he muttered gloomily, "I see it all now! What a pig I have been! A pig – that's me! Just a pig – a plain pig!"

He waited till Mole's sobs became gradually less stormy and more rhythmical; he waited till at last sniffs were frequent and sobs only intermittent. Then he rose from his seat, and, remarking carelessly, "Well, now we'd really better be getting on, old chap!" set off up the road again over the toilsome way they had come.

"Wherever are you (hic) going to (hic), Ratty?" cried the tearful Mole, looking up in alarm.

"We're going to find that home of yours, old fellow," replied the Rat pleasantly; "so you had better come along, for it will take some finding, and we shall want your nose."

Kenneth Grahame

Nicolette says:

Edith Cavell was a British nurse, and a spy during the First World War. She helped some two hundred Allied soldiers escape from German-occupied Belgium, for which she was court-martialled, found guilty of treason and executed. She spoke these words on the night before her execution, on 12 October 1915.

This is one of my favourite inscriptions on a statue. It stands at the foot of St Martin's Lane, in London. As I write, I resolve to lay flowers there next 12 October.

Patriotism is not enough. I must have no hatred or bitterness for anyone.

Edith Cavell

Chapter 6

On Equality and Justice

Contents

Nicolette says:

These words come from a speech given by Michelle Obama, the first African-American First Lady of the United States.

Two strong arguments for exercising your democratic right to vote are: the history of how hard-won it was, particularly for women (but widespread men's suffrage was a long time coming too) and the fact that it is our best instrument for change. Encourage the adults around you to vote, and don't waste your chance when it comes.

From

TUSKGEE UNIVERSITY COMMENCEMENT ADDRESS

You've got to vote, vote, vote.

That's it; that's the way we move forward.

Michelle Obama

Nicolette says:

Mary Wollstonecraft (1759–1797) was a writer and champion of the rights of women. She was one the earliest feminist philosophers, and the work from which these words are taken, A Vindication of the Rights of Women, published in 1792, is considered to be one of the first feminist texts.

From

A VINDICATION OF THE RIGHTS OF WOMEN

I lament that women are systematically degraded by receiving the trivial attentions, which men think it manly to pay to the sex, when, in fact, they are insultingly supporting their own superiority.

Mary Wollstonecraft

Nicolette says:

The echo between the pioneer of women's rights and freedoms, Mary Wollstonecraft, writing in 1792, and Laura Bates, founder of the Everyday Sexism movement, writing in 2014, gives me pause.

It turns out that women have been saying the same thing about unasked-for compliments from men for more than 200 years, and it is still necessary to say it.

From
THE GUARDIAN

[On unasked-for attention in the street]
I don't take it as a compliment. Because it's not a compliment. It's a statement of power. It's a way of letting me know that a man has the right to my body, a right to discuss it, analyse it, appraise it, and let me or anybody else in the vicinity know his verdict, whether I like it or not.

Laura Bates

Nicolette says:

Laura Bates invited women and men to
offer their experience of discrimination,
harassment and assault on a website, and
found 50,000 instances were posted in the
first eighteen months. She herself became
the target of appalling aggression online,
including rape threats. She has since worked
with the police and other authorities to use the
patterns revealed by her data to help to deter
and prosecute perpetrators.

Feminism means believing that everybody should be treated equally regardless of their sex.

Laura Bates

Nicolette says:

X González was eighteen years old
when they survived the shooting at
Marjory Stoneman Douglas High School
in Parkland, Florida on 14 February 2018.
Seventeen students and staff members were
killed and seventeen more injured by a former
student. González and friends founded the
gun-control advocacy body Never Again, and,
with fellow students, led the March for Our Lives
in Washington DC on 24 March 2018, with
a turnout of an estimated two million people,
one of the largest protests in American history.
Among the many speakers — survivors and family
of survivors of shootings — González spoke and
then fell silent for some minutes. They revealed
that the time between them starting to speak
and the end of the silence was six minutes and
twenty seconds — the length of time it took
for the victims in their school to be shot.

González is proof of what young people
can achieve. Though their fight is not over.
Shootings still happen.

From
A SPEECH BY X GONZÁLEZ

We are speaking up for those who don't have anyone listening to them, for those who can't talk about it just yet, and for those who will never speak again. We are grieving, we are furious, and we are using our words fiercely and desperately because that's the only thing standing between us and this happening again.

I knew that . . . we were going to be the people who were going to make that change . . . we were going to be the ones who were going out into Congress and telling them, this is our fight now because you messed it up so badly that you left it to the kids and now it's our job.

X González

Nicolette says:

This, from Dr. Seuss's picture-book collection
Yertle the Turtle and Other Stories, is the voice
of rebellion, from an ordinary turtle called Mack,
who is at the bottom of a big pile of turtles
that King Yertle has piled his throne on. King
Yertle believes that he rules everything he can
see, and the higher his throne, the more powerful
he is. But, as is always the case when rulers will
do anything to add to their power, ordinary
creatures suffer. Seuss makes this idea simple
in his splendid, rhythmic story.

Consider who you are sitting on in order to add
to your power. And if you are being sat on, try
shaking things up. (Mack does it by burping, but
do whatever dislodges the tyrant.)

You can read more from Dr. Seuss on page 235.

From

YERTLE THE TURTLE AND OTHER STORIES

I know, up at top,

you are seeing great sights

But down at the bottom

we, too, should have rights.

Dr. Seuss

Nicolette says:

Standing in front of the
Lincoln Memorial in Washington DC
in 1963, Dr Martin Luther King, Jr.
(1929–1968) gave a speech about
civil rights and racial equality.
It included these words.

This is one of the most famous speeches of
modern history, using the language and
rhythms of the church pulpit — King was a
Baptist minister — to sing out for racial equality.

From

Address Delivered at the March On Washington For Jobs And Freedom

Even though we face the difficulties of today and tomorrow, I still have a dream. It is a dream deeply rooted in the American dream.

I have a dream that one day this nation will rise up and live out the true meaning of its creed: "We hold these truths to be self-evident, that all men are created equal."

I have a dream that one day on the red hills of Georgia, the sons of former slaves and the sons of former slave owners will be able to sit down together at the table of brotherhood.

I have a dream that one day even the state of Mississippi, a state sweltering with the heat of injustice, sweltering with the heat of oppression, will be transformed into an oasis of freedom and justice.

I have a dream that my four little children will one day live in a nation where they will not be judged by the color of their skin but by the content of their character. I have a dream today.

I have a dream that one day down in Alabama, with its vicious racists, with its governor having his lips dripping with the words of "interposition" and "nullification", one day right there in Alabama little black boys and black girls will be able to join hands with little white boys and white girls as sisters and brothers. I have a dream today.

I have a dream that one day every valley shall be exalted, every hill and mountain shall be made low, the rough places will be made plain, and the crooked places will be made straight, and the glory of the Lord shall be revealed, and all flesh shall see it together.

This is our hope. This is the faith that I go back to the South with. With this faith we will be able to hew out of the mountain of despair a stone of hope. With this faith we will be able to transform the jangling discords of our nation into a beautiful symphony of brotherhood. With this faith we will be able to work together, to pray together, to struggle together, to go to jail together, to stand up for freedom together, knowing that we will be free one day.

This will be the day, this will be the day when all of God's children will be able to sing with new meaning: "My country, 'tis of thee, sweet land of liberty, of thee I sing. Land where my fathers died, land of the pilgrim's pride, from every mountainside, let freedom ring!"

And if America is to be a great nation, this must become true. So let freedom ring from the prodigious hilltops of New Hampshire. Let freedom ring from the mighty mountains of New York. Let freedom ring from the heightening Alleghenies of Pennsylvania. Let freedom ring from the snow-capped Rockies of Colorado. Let freedom ring from the curvaceous slopes of California. But not only that: Let freedom ring from Stone Mountain of Georgia. Let freedom ring from Lookout Mountain of Tennessee. Let freedom ring from every hill and molehill of Mississippi. From every mountainside, let freedom ring.

And when this happens, and when we allow freedom to ring, when we let it ring from every village and every hamlet, from every state and every city, we will be able to speed up that day when all of God's children, black men and white men, Jews and Gentiles, Protestants and Catholics, will be able to join hands and sing in the words of the old Negro spiritual: "Free at last! Free at last! Thank God Almighty, we are free at last!"

Dr Martin Luther King, Jr.

Nicolette says:

The British philosopher Bertrand Russell
(1872–1970) summed things up here, for his
lifetime and most certainly for now. Russell was an
anti-war activist and pacifist, and went to prison
for his pacifism during the First World War.

Love is wise – Hatred is foolish. In this world, which is getting more and more closely interconnected, we have to learn to tolerate each other. We have to learn to put up with the fact that some people say things we don't like. We can only live together in that way. But if we are to live together, and not die together, we must learn a kind of charity and a kind of tolerance which is absolutely vital to the continuation of human life on this planet.

Bertrand Russell

Nicolette says:

Malala Yousafzai and two of her friends were shot
on a bus by a Taliban gunman on 9 October 2012
in retaliation for their activism around education
for girls in Pakistan. She had been writing an
anonymous blog since she was eleven, and had
appeared in an American documentary and
been interviewed in print and on television.
She was fifteen when she was wounded.

The speech from which the words opposite are
extracted was given less than a year later, on her
sixteenth birthday, and gave rise to a movement
for universal education. At seventeen, Malala
became the youngest-ever recipient of a
Nobel Prize for Peace.

From

SPEECH AT THE UNITED NATIONS

Dear sisters and brothers, we realise the importance of light when we see darkness. We realise the importance of our voice when we are silenced. In the same way, when we were in Swat, the north of Pakistan, we realised the importance of pens and books when we saw the guns.

The wise saying, "The pen is mightier than the sword" was true. The extremists are afraid of books and pens. The power of education frightens them. They are afraid of women. The power of the voice of women frightens them.

I remember that there was a boy in our school who was asked by a journalist, "Why are the Taliban against education?" He answered very simply. By pointing to his book he said, "A Talib doesn't know what is written inside this book." They think that God is a tiny, little conservative being who would send girls to hell just because of going to school. The terrorists are misusing the name of Islam and Pashtun society for their own personal benefits. Pakistan is a peace-loving democratic country. Pashtuns want education for their daughters and sons. And Islam is a religion of peace, humanity and brotherhood. Islam says that it is not only each child's right to get education, rather it is their duty and responsibility.

Dear brothers and sisters, we must not forget that millions of people are suffering from poverty, injustice and ignorance. We must not forget that millions of children are out of their schools. We must not forget that our sisters and brothers are waiting for a bright, peaceful future.

So let us wage a global struggle against illiteracy, poverty and terrorism and let us pick up our books and pens. They are our most powerful weapons.

One child, one teacher, one pen and one book can change the world.

Education is the only solution. Education first.

Malala Yousafzai

Nicolette says:

Jo Cox (1974–2016), who was elected to parliament in 2015, gave her first speech in the House of Commons Chamber on 3 June 2015. On 16 June 2016, she died after being shot and stabbed multiple times outside the library in Birstall, near Leeds, where she was about to meet constituents. Her killer is in prison for life.

Jo's words gave rise to the More in Common movement, to bring communities together with street parties, gatherings, events and campaigns. Jo's beliefs gave us all something, even after her death. Her killer did nothing but take away.

Our communities have been deeply enhanced by immigration, be it of Irish Catholics across the constituency or of Muslims from Gujarat in India or from Pakistan, principally from Kashmir. While we celebrate our diversity, what surprises me time and time again as I travel around the constituency is that we are far more united and have far more in common with each other than things that divide us.

Jo Cox

Nicolette says:

I first discovered this poem on the wall of a
children's acting class, run by the inspirational
drama teacher Anna Scher. Pastor Niemöller was
one of her heroes. It is a simple message, to speak
out for each other when we are not threatened
ourselves, but it is not easy to put into practice.
Niemöller, a Protestant, not a Jew, survived
seven years in a concentration camp for
opposing the Nazis.

FIRST THEY CAME...

First they came for the socialists, and I did not
speak out –
> Because I was not a socialist.

Then they came for the trade unionists, and I
did not speak out –
> Because I was not a trade unionist.

Then they came for the Jews, and I did not
speak out –
> Because I was not a Jew.

Then they came for me – and there was
no one left to speak for me.

Pastor Martin Niemöller

Nicolette says:

Desmond Tutu, the South African cleric, human rights activist and anti-apartheid campaigner who was the first Black African to hold the position of Archbishop of Cape Town, puts his point about injustice very clearly here, which makes it seem simple. But it is hard to act on. Staying out of it is easier. It is also damaging. Be brave and free the mouse.

Neutrality can be a good thing, but only if we use it actively to make both sides safe, and to make peace between them. Involvement matters.

If you are neutral in situations of injustice,
you have chosen the side of the oppressor.
If an elephant has its foot on the tail of
a mouse and you say that you are
neutral, the mouse will not appreciate
your neutrality.

Desmond Tutu

Nicolette says:

Some children are unlucky enough to experience war first-hand. But for so many of us, this is how we encounter it — on a screen that can be switched off, or switched over. This poem, by the writer Hilary McKay, reminds us of our responsibility for what happens when we are not watching.

WAR AND THE SIMPSONS

The really good thing about war is that
       they generally put it on at 6 o'clock.
Same time as *The Simpsons*

And nowadays, of course, war is quite safe.
It stays in the TV and makes no mess.
Even if it gets too noisy you can just
       turn down the sound.

(If you can find the remote.)

Also it is very clean,

No dust, nor smoke, nor blood leaks

through the screen.

And when it gets boring you can switch over

and watch *The Simpsons*

(If you can find the remote.)

The only trouble is, it still goes on.

(The war, not *The Simpsons*. *The Simpsons*

lasts for twenty minutes –

unless it is a special.)

The war still goes on.

The noise and the smoke and the leaking blood.

The dirt and the boredom and the fear.

You cannot switch it off with the remote.

(Even if you can find the remote.)

You have to switch it off another way
You have to say, No
No
No war
You have to say No To War.

Then you can watch *The Simpsons*
In peace.

Hilary McKay

Nicolette says:

Words for us all from Barack Obama,
the 44th President of the United States, and the
first African-American to be elected President.
The theme of "change" was a key message during
Obama's first presidential election campaign,
and this quotation comes from a speech he
gave in February 2008.

Change will not come if we wait for some other person or if we wait for some other time. We are the ones we've been waiting for. We are the change that we seek.

Barack Obama

Nicolette says:

Anne Frank was a Jewish girl who had to hide from the occupying Nazis in an attic in Amsterdam, in the Netherlands, during the Second World War, with her family and other people, and who kept a diary while she was there (1942–1944), from the age of thirteen. The attic was discovered, and its occupants sent to concentration camps where Anne died, at fifteen, not long before the end of the war. Her father, the only surviving member of her family, later returned to the attic and found that his secretary and their protector, Miep Gies, had kept Anne's diary, which went on to be published in seventy languages. Anne's voice is full of defiance and hope and the emotions of adolescence, and her thoughts have had a huge impact on the world.

Remember Anne Frank if you think you might be too young to make a difference.

From
THE DIARY OF
A YOUNG GIRL

We aren't allowed to have an opinion ... Not have an opinion! People can tell you to shut up, but they can't keep you from having an opinion. You can't forbid someone to have an opinion, no matter how young they are!

From
TALES FROM
THE SECRET ANNEXE

How wonderful it is that no one has to wait, but can start right now to gradually change the world!

Anne Frank

Nicolette says:

Harvey Milk, who was gay, campaigned against discrimination on the grounds of sexual orientation in California in the 1970s. He was assassinated at the age of forty-eight.

If your environment does not feel safe and supportive, find someone you trust to talk to.

All young people, regardless of sexual orientation or identity, deserve a safe and supportive environment in which to achieve their full potential.

Harvey Milk

Nicolette says:

Education should always be the weedkiller of prejudice. Ignorance feeds it.

These words come from Jane Eyre by Charlotte Brontë (1816–1855), published in 1847. It was one of the very first novels to use a first-person narrative, which gives us particular insight into Jane's state of mind.

Like the books by Charlotte's sisters, Emily and Anne Brontë, Jane Eyre was originally published under a male pseudonym. Charlotte's was Currer Bell.

From
JANE EYRE

Prejudices, it is well known, are most difficult to eradicate from the heart whose soil has never been loosened or fertilised by education; they grow there firm as weeds among stones.

Charlotte Brontë

Nicolette says:

Claudette Colvin is a retired American nurse aide who was a pioneer of the Civil Rights Movement and a forerunner of Rosa Parks (whose words you can read on page 113). At the age of only fifteen, in 1955, she was arrested in Montgomery, Alabama, for refusing to give up her seat to a white woman on a crowded, segregated bus.

Tim Minchin's song Naughty, from Matilda: The Musical, which you can read on page 107, also echoes Colvin's sentiment.

I knew then and I know now that, when it comes to justice, there is no easy way to get it. You can't sugarcoat it. You have to take a stand and say, "This is not right."

Claudette Colvin

Nicolette says:

Never think that it doesn't matter whether things are true or not. Find out the difference. Don't believe anything (especially in this age of social media) that you can't verify. Spread only the truth, and never the falsehoods.

Ida B. Wells (1862–1931) was an American investigative journalist and an early leader in the Civil Rights Movement.

From

THE LIGHT OF TRUTH: WRITINGS OF AN ANTI-LYNCHING CRUSADER

The way to right wrongs is to
turn the light of truth upon them.

Ida B. Wells

Nicolette says:

We talk of being blinded by love, and of
blind terror. But James Baldwin (1924–1987),
the great American writer, poet and activist,
is right, in these words, taken from his novel
If Beale Street Could Talk. Not to care is
not to notice. Care enough to see what matters.

From
If Beale Street Could Talk

Neither love nor terror makes one blind:
indifference makes one blind.

James Baldwin

Nicolette says:

Eric Garner died in New York City in 2014, after police officers tried to arrest him on suspicion of a minor offence — selling single, untaxed cigarettes — and put him in a chokehold (which was subsequently banned). Before he died he said, eleven times, "I can't breathe" — words which became a rallying cry for those protesting against the harassment and murder of Black people by police.

Ross Gay is an award-winning American poet and professor.

A SMALL NEEDFUL FACT

Is that Eric Garner worked
for some time for the Parks and Rec.
Horticultural Department, which means,
perhaps, that with his very large hands,
perhaps, in all likelihood,
he put gently into the earth
some plants which, most likely,
some of them, in all likelihood,
continue to grow, continue
to do what such plants do, like house
and feed small and necessary creatures,
like being pleasant to touch and smell,
like converting sunlight
into food, like making it easier
for us to breathe.

Ross Gay

Chapter 7

ON READING

Contents

Nicolette says:

The History Boys is a play for grown-ups,
by Leeds-born playwright Alan Bennett, about
a group of schoolboys and an unconventional
teacher, Hector. This thought, about how reading
can work, is one of the best expressions of its
potential I have ever heard.

From
THE HISTORY BOYS

The best moments in reading are when you come across something – a thought, a feeling, a way of looking at things – which you had thought special and particular to you.
Now here it is, set down by someone else, a person you have never met, someone even who is long dead. And it is as if a hand has come out and taken yours.

Alan Bennett

Nicolette says:

"Must be magic", comedian Bo Burnham
writes about the act of reading. Indeed it must.
Stop for a moment, as Burnham has made us do
in this poem, to think about the strangeness of
translating marks on a page into voices in your
head. And what is more, into pictures. When you
(silently) do the crotchety-old-man voice, do you
see him, or see yourself scrunching yourself up
to be like him? Yes, thought so. So do I. Never
forget how fantastically weird reading is.

Magic

Read this to yourself. Read it silently.

Don't move your lips. Don't make a sound.

Listen to yourself.

Listen without hearing anything.

What a wonderfully weird thing, huh?

NOW MAKE THIS PART LOUD!

SCREAM IT IN YOUR MIND!

DROWN EVERYTHING OUT.

Now, hear a whisper. A tiny whisper.

Now, read this next line with your best crotchety-old-man voice:
"Hello there, sonny. Does your town have a post office?"
Awesome! Who was that? Whose voice was that?
It sure wasn't yours!

How do you do that?
How?!
Must be magic.

Bo Burnham

Nicolette says:

Reading is not a passive activity. Using your imagination is creative. Unleash it when you read. Picture the scenes.

This extract is from I Capture the Castle, the first novel by Dodie Smith (1896–1990), who later became famous for her book The Hundred and One Dalmatians. I Capture the Castle was published in 1948, and written during the Second World War, when Smith was living in California, having moved from England, and was missing her home country.

From

I CAPTURE THE CASTLE

When I read a book, I put in all the imagination I can, so that it is almost like writing the book as well as reading it – or rather, it is like living it. It makes reading so much more exciting, but I don't suppose many people try to do it.

Dodie Smith

Nicolette says:

Dr. Seuss (real name: Theodor Geisel) understood the magic of reading. And his long, silly, rhythmic illustrated poems, such as Green Eggs and Ham and The Cat in the Hat, were specifically designed with limited vocabulary to help children learn to sound out letters and acquire the skill of reading. They were keys to open the doors.

You can read more from Dr. Seuss on page 179.

From

I CAN READ WITH MY EYES SHUT

The more that you read, the more things
you will know.
The more that you learn, the more places
you'll go.

Dr. Seuss

Nicolette says:

The best way to experience something outside your own life is through stories. Non-readers limit themselves.

These words are from the fifth book in author George R.R. Martin's fantasy series A Song of Fire and Ice, which began with A Game of Thrones.

From

A DANCE WITH DRAGONS

A reader lives a thousand lives before he dies. . .
The man who never reads lives only one.

George R.R. Martin

Nicolette says:

Books literally open like doors — and, as author Katherine Rundell says here, in her novel Rooftoppers, they also work like levers, forcing your way into places (and opportunities) that are otherwise locked to you.

You can find more things to read from Katherine Rundell on pages 141 and 245.

From

ROOFTOPPERS

Books crowbar the world open for you.

Katherine Rundell

Nicolette says:

Ursula K. Le Guin (1929–2018) wrote fantasy and science fiction for adults, and twelve books for children. You might start with The Wizard of Earthsea, to find out how she made the truth that she describes here happen in her own writing.

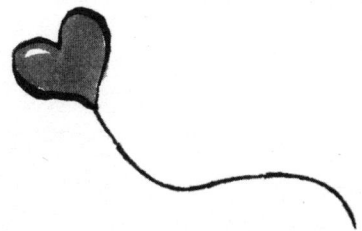

From

THE LANGUAGE OF THE NIGHT: ESSAYS ON FANTASY AND SCIENCE FICTION

We read books to find out who we are. What other people, real or imaginary, do and think and feel . . . is an essential guide to our understanding of what we ourselves are and may become.

Ursula K. Le Guin

Nicolette says:

Not every book makes every reader feel like
Frances Hodgson Burnett's Sara, described here
in A Little Princess. We are allowed to dislike a
book. But if we dislike all books it's because we
haven't yet found the right book for us at the
right time. Or because somebody has made
reading an unhappy experience for us. That is the
fault of the somebody, and not the fault of books.
And that somebody must not be allowed to win
by stealing the pleasure of reading from you.
If reading aloud, or reading what you are told
to read, or in order to be tested on it, or in
competition with other readers, is no fun for you,
or you are jeered at or sneered at for liking to
read: read secretly. Read subversively. Read what
you choose, anything you like, without telling
anyone you are doing it. Then it is just between
you and the book. (Or listen to it: audio counts.)
Your pleasure is all your own, for no one to ruin.
Take reading back from the spoilers.
Make it yours. And don't let on.

You can read more from Frances Hodgson Burnett
on page 77.

From

A LITTLE PRINCESS

Never did she find anything so difficult as to keep herself from losing her temper when she was suddenly disturbed while absorbed in a book. People who are fond of books know the feeling of irritation which sweeps over them at such a moment. The temptation to be unreasonable and snappish is one not easy to manage.

Frances Hodgson Burnett

Nicolette says:

When you find the right book, it can feel
just as Katherine Rundell describes here.

You can find more things to read from
Katherine Rundell on pages 141 and 239.

Reading is almost exactly like a cartwheel;
it turns the world upside down and leaves
you breathless.

Katherine Rundell

Nicolette says:

A moment featuring the eccentric, elderly
Miss Prothero, in poet and writer Dylan Thomas's
funny, nostalgic memoir of a Welsh childhood,
A Child's Christmas in Wales, which was
originally written as a radio broadcast in 1952,
and later published in 1955. Miss Prothero is
both absurd, and recognises what is important.

From

A Child's Christmas in Wales

And when the firemen turned off the hose and were standing in the wet, smoky room, Jim's aunt, Miss Prothero, came downstairs and peered in at them.

Jim and I waited, very quietly, to hear what she would say to them. She said the right thing, always. She looked at the three tall firemen in their shining helmets, standing among the smoke and cinders and dissolving snowballs, and she said, "Would you like anything to read?"

Dylan Thomas

Nicolette says:

This is the description of a sleeping compartment on an overnight train.

When I was at junior school my friend Alison knew this whole poem by heart and we walked around the playground together with her teaching it to me, line by line. I went home and recited it. My parents found me the book, Old Possum's Book of Practical Cats, and I learned, over the next few years, many more of Eliot's cat poems, which I still remember.

Sleeping compartments on trains are rarer now than they used to be, but I was lucky enough to experience them, and always delighted in the "funny little basin you're supposed to wash your face in". And what is especially magical about this poem is that it recreates the rhythm of the train, at two speeds.

It is a soothing rhythm. Having this in my head has got me through scary times, and dentists' appointments.

From

SKIMBLESHANKS THE RAILWAY CAT

Oh, it's very pleasant when

you have found your little den

With your name written up on the door.

And the berth is very neat

with a newly folded sheet

And there's not a speck of dust on the floor.

There is every sort of light—

you can make it dark or bright;

There's a handle that you turn to make a breeze.

There's a funny little basin

you're supposed to wash your face in

And a crank to shut the window if you sneeze.

Then the guard looks in politely

     and will ask you very brightly

"Do you like your morning tea weak or strong?"

But Skimble's just behind him

     and was ready to remind him,

For Skimble won't let anything go wrong.

      And when you creep into your cosy berth

        And pull up the counterpane,

You ought to reflect that it's very nice

To know that you won't be bothered by mice—

      You can leave all that to the Railway Cat,

       The Cat of the Railway Train!

T.S. Eliot

Chapter 8

On
Becoming
You and
Your
Future

Contents

Nicolette says:

This passage comes from Louisa May Alcott's coming-of-age novel Little Women, published in 1868, which is set during the American Civil War and tells the story of the lives of the four March sisters: Meg, Jo, Beth and Amy. Despite the goodness of Meg (the eldest of the four March women), it is Jo – the brave, outspoken, headstrong sister, and the one who is speaking here – who has always been the one to identify with.

From
LITTLE WOMEN

I want to do something splendid . . .
something heroic or wonderful that won't
be forgotten after I'm dead. I don't know
what, but I'm on the watch for it and mean
to astonish you all some day.

Louisa May Alcott

Nicolette says:

The joy of youth is that there is plenty of time
to make a difference to the world if you want to.

These lyrics are from the song The Room Where
It Happens, from Hamilton: The Musical, the
stage musical written by Lin-Manuel Miranda,
which tells the story of Alexander Hamilton,
one of the Founding Fathers of the United States.
The song depicts the events of the Compromise
of 1790, the historical political agreement
which would shape the future of the country.

You can find more to read from
Lin-Manuel Miranda on page 267.

From

HAMILTON: THE MUSICAL

God help and forgive me

I wanna build

Something that's gonna

Outlive me

Lin-Manuel Miranda

Nicolette says:

*Simple and effective: a poem
against preconceptions.*

You can read more from
Benjamin Zephaniah on page 147.

WHO'S WHO

I used to think nurses

Were women,

I used to think police

Were men,

I used to think poets

Were boring,

Until I became one of them.

Benjamin Zephaniah

Nicolette says:

I love this little poem because it tells us that those who aspire to power don't always have anything to offer when they achieve it.

THE LEADER

I wanna be the leader
I wanna be the leader
Can I be the leader?
Can I? I can?
Promise? Promise?
Yippee I'm the leader
I'm the leader

OK what shall we do?

Roger McGough

Nicolette says:

Seneca, the Roman philosopher and dramatist, lived more than 2,000 years ago, and said this in Latin. It is no less true now, in English.

As is a tale, so is life:

not how long it is,

but how good it is,

is what matters.

Seneca

Nicolette says:

These lyrics are from the song Wait For It,
from Hamilton: The Musical, the stage musical
written by Lin-Manuel Miranda. They are spoken
by Aaron Burr, the third Vice President of the
United States, who killed Alexander Hamilton,
the former Secretary of the Treasury, in a duel
in 1804, after a long rivalry between the two
men. Burr is a deeply flawed character, but he
sings of hope. Even if we don't manage to lead
the good life that Seneca describes in the
previous passage, "Life doesn't discriminate
between the sinners and the saints", and we
have to keep living anyway. Nor is there any
reason to rush towards our future.

You can find more to read from Lin-Manuel Miranda
on page 259.

From

HAMILTON: THE MUSICAL

I'm willing to wait for it . . .

Life doesn't discriminate

Between the sinners and the saints

It takes and it takes and it takes

And we keep living anyway

We rise and we fall and we break

And we make our mistakes

And if there's a reason I'm still alive

When so many have died

Then I'm willin' to—

Wait for it

Lin-Manuel Miranda

Nicolette says:

Stephen Hawking (1942–2018) was a scientist and professor of mathematics who lived with physical limitations caused by motor neurone disease for more than fifty years, and understood the complex physics of space. His lessons for life are ones anyone can grasp.

Here are the most important pieces of advice that I've passed on to my children . . .

One, remember to look up at the stars and not down at your feet.

Two, never give up work. Work gives you meaning and purpose and life is empty without it.

Three, if you are lucky enough to find love, remember it is rare and don't throw it away.

Stephen Hawking

Nicolette says:

My secondary school motto was Age Quod Agis —
"Do What You Do", often translated at the time
as "Do Your Thing". At twelve, I thought it was
rather silly, but since then I have come to believe
it is infinitely wise. The secret of life is to find
your thing, and then get on and do it. These
remarks from Steve Jobs, the co-founder of
Apple Inc., to students graduating from
university reminded me of this. Those who
find their thing are fortunate, because then
they can concentrate on a way to do it. And
if you love doing it you will be more likely to
overcome hurdles, and have a better time
in the attempt. Good luck with the search.

From

STANFORD COMMENCEMENT ADDRESS

I'm convinced that the only thing that kept me going was that I loved what I did. You've got to find what you love.

Steve Jobs

Nicolette says:

Life is full of choices that affect everything that happens afterwards, but we can't know what all the effects will be when we make the choice.

I look back on my life (so far) and can see places where the roads diverged. I like my life, but sometimes I think about all the things that would have been different if I had gone another way, and I wonder.

This poem is about taking the less common and conventional path. That is a basis on which to make a choice, but life will always involve leaps in the dark.

The Road Not Taken

Two roads diverged in a yellow wood,
And sorry I could not travel both
And be one traveler, long I stood
And looked down one as far as I could
To where it bent in the undergrowth;

Then took the other, as just as fair,
And having perhaps the better claim,
Because it was grassy and wanted wear;
Though as for that the passing there
Had worn them really about the same,

And both that morning equally lay

In leaves no step had trodden black.

Oh, I kept the first for another day!

Yet knowing how way leads on to way,

I doubted if I should ever come back.

I shall be telling this with a sigh

Somewhere ages and ages hence:

Two roads diverged in a wood, and I—

I took the one less traveled by,

And that has made all the difference.

Robert Frost

Nicolette says:

This comes from a novel from 1912 for
young adults, Daddy-Long-Legs,
written by Jean Webster.

Young people are naturally more imaginative
than most adults. Children's play involves so much
make-believe. But as we get older we may stop
exercising our imagination, and then it weakens.
Keep making up stories — either writing them
down, or in your head. You can practise by
watching strangers and imagining what their
lives are like, or listening to other people and
visualising what they tell you about. Or read
stories — true or fictional — and conjure in your
mind the scenes they describe, and guess what
will happen next. I used to write stories a lot as
a child, and then I started to write essays instead.
I wish I had done more to keep training
my imagination.

But it's not too late for you.

From

DADDY-LONG-LEGS

The most necessary quality for any person to have is imagination. It makes people able to put themselves in other people's places. It makes them kind and sympathetic and understanding. It ought to be cultivated in children.

Jean Webster

Nicolette says:

Frances Hardinge's books are full of wisdom.
In this fantasy adventure, Deeplight, her
observation is true, that other people influence us
all the time. But we don't have to copy them or
do as they say. There are always options.

Think about the ways people might be
changing you, and choose what you are
willing to go along with.

You can find more to read from Frances Hardinge
on page 49.

From

DEEPLIGHT

We are all squeezed into new shapes
by the people around us. If we are
paying attention, though, we always
have some say in how we are altered.

Frances Hardinge

Nicolette says:

Is this the most poignant passage in children's
literature? Some find Winnie-the-Pooh
too cute, but this is about growing up, and is
a moving reminder of, and tribute to, what we
leave behind. Everyone goes through it — perhaps
that is why it is so popular. And when we are
grown up, in our hearts the children we were will
always be playing.

THE HOUSE AT POOH CORNER

Then, suddenly again, Christopher Robin, who was still looking at the world with his chin in his hands, called out "Pooh!"

"Yes?" said Pooh.

"When I'm – when – Pooh!"

"Yes, Christopher Robin?"

"I'm not going to do Nothing any more."

"Never again?"

"Well, not so much. They don't let you."

Pooh waited for him to go on, but he was silent again.

"Yes, Christopher Robin?" said Pooh helpfully.

"Pooh, when I'm – you know – when I'm not doing Nothing, will you come up here sometimes?"

"Just me?"

"Yes, Pooh."

"Will you be here too?"

"Yes, Pooh, I will be, really. I promise I will be, Pooh."

"That's good," said Pooh.

"Pooh, promise you won't forget about me, ever. Not even when I'm a hundred."

Pooh thought for a little.

"How old shall I be then?"

"Ninety-nine."

Pooh nodded.

"I promise," he said.

Still with his eyes on the world
Christopher Robin put out a hand and
felt for Pooh's paw.

"Pooh," said Christopher Robin earnestly,
"if I – if I'm not quite –" he stopped and
tried again – "Pooh, whatever happens,
you will understand, won't you?"

"Understand what?"

"Oh, nothing." He laughed and jumped to
his feet. "Come on!"

"Where?" said Pooh.

"Anywhere," said Christopher Robin.

So they went off together. But wherever they go, and whatever happens to them on the way, in that enchanted place on the top of the Forest a little boy and his Bear will always be playing.

A.A. Milne

INDEX

Index of Authors

Acknowledgements

James Baldwin: Extract from IF BEALE STREET COULD TALK by James Baldwin, first published by Michael Joseph 1974, copyright © James Baldwin 1974. **Laura Bates:** Extract from theguardian.com, 28 February 2014, "Women should not accept street harassment as a compliment", copyright Guardian News & Media Ltd 2020. Quotation by Laura Bates, copyright © Laura Bates. **Alan Bennett:** (UK & Canada) Extract from THE HISTORY BOYS by Alan Bennett, Faber and Faber 2004, reprinted by permission of Faber and Faber Ltd. (US) Extract from THE HISTORY BOYS by Alan Bennett (© Forelake Ltd 2004) is printed by permission of United Agents (www.unitedagents.co.uk) on behalf of Forelake Ltd. **Michael Bond:** Extract from A BEAR CALLED PADDINGTON, reprinted by permission of HarperCollins Publishers Ltd, © Michael Bond 1958. **Bill Bryson:** (UK) Extract from THE BODY by Bill Bryson published by Doubleday. Copyright © Bill Bryson 2019. Reprinted by permission of The Random House Group Limited. (US) Excerpt from THE BODY: A GUIDE FOR OCCUPANTS by Bill Bryson, copyright © 2019 by Bill Bryson. Used by permission of Doubleday, an imprint of the Knopf Doubleday Publishing Group, a division of Penguin Random House LLC. All rights reserved. (Canada) Excerpt from THE BODY: A GUIDE FOR OCCUPANTS by Bill Bryson. Copyright © 2019 Bill Bryson. Reprinted by permission of Doubleday Canada, a division of Penguin Random House Canada Limited. All rights reserved. **Bo Burnham:** "Magic" from EGGHEAD: OR, YOU CAN'T SURVIVE ON IDEAS ALONE, Orion 2013, copyright © Bo Burnham 2013, reprinted by permission of Hachette Book Group. **Claudette Colvin:** Quotation by Claudette Colvin, www.biography.com/activist/claudette-colvin. **Jo Cox:** Extract from Jo Cox MP's maiden speech to Parliament, 3 June 2015. Contains Parliamentary information licensed under the Open Parliament Licence v3.0. **Roald Dahl:** (World ebook and UK print) Extract from DANNY THE CHAMPION OF THE WORLD by Roald Dahl, Jonathan Cape and Penguin Books Ltd 1975, copyright © Roald Dahl Story Company Ltd, 1975, reprinted by permission of David Higham Associates. (US & Canada print) Excerpt from DANNY THE CHAMPION OF THE WORLD by Roald Dahl, copyright © 1975 by Roald Dahl Nominee Limited. Used by permission of Alfred A. Knopf, an imprint of Random House Children's Books, a division of Penguin Random House LLC. All rights reserved. **Gerald Durrell:** Extract from ENCOUNTERS WITH ANIMALS, reproduced with permission of Curtis Brown

Group Ltd, London, on behalf of the Beneficiaries of The Estate of Gerald Durrell. Copyright © Gerald Durrell 1958. **Albert Einstein:** Extract from an interview with G. S. Viereck, "What Life Means to Einstein," Saturday Evening Post, October 26, 1929, © The Hebrew University of Jerusalem, reprinted by permission of The Albert Einstein Archives, The Hebrew University of Jerusalem. **T.S. Eliot:** (UK & Canada) Extract from "Skimbleshanks the Railway Cat" from OLD POSSUM'S BOOK OF PRACTICAL CATS by T.S. Eliot, Faber and Faber 1939, reprinted by permission of Faber and Faber Ltd. (US) "Skimbleshanks: The Railway Cat" from OLD POSSUM'S BOOK OF PRACTICAL CATS by T.S. Eliot. Copyright 1939 by T.S. Eliot and renewed 1967 by Esme Valerie Eliot. Reprinted by permission of Clarion Books, an imprint of HarperCollins Publishers. All rights reserved. **Roger Federer:** Quotation by Roger Federer, US Open, 2017. **John Finnemore:** Tweet by John Finnemore (© Since You Ask Me Ltd, 2012) is printed by permission of United Agents (www.unitedagents.co.uk) on behalf of John Finnemore. **Anne Frank:** (UK) Forty-two (42) words from THE DIARY OF A YOUNG GIRL by Anne Frank, translated by Mirjam Pressler and Susan Massotty (Viking, 1997) copyright © The Anne Frank-Fonds, Basel, Switzerland, 1991. English translation copyright © Doubleday a division of Bantam Doubleday Dell Publishing Group Inc, 1995. Reprinted by permission of Penguin Books Limited. Extract from ANNE FRANK'S TALES FROM THE SECRET ANNEXE by Anne Frank, Halban Publishers Ltd. London 2010. Copyright © 1949, 1960 by Otto Frank. Copyright © 1982, 2003, 2010 by Anne Frank-Fonds, Basel. English Translation copyright © 2003, 2010 by Susan Massotty. Reprinted by permission of Halban Publishers. (US & Canada) Excerpt from THE DIARY OF A YOUNG GIRL: THE DEFINITIVE EDITION by Anne Frank, edited by Otto H. Frank and Mirjam Pressler, translated by Susan Massotty, translation copyright © 1995 by Penguin Random House LLC; excerpt from ANNE FRANK'S TALES FROM THE SECRET ANNEX: A COLLECTION OF HER SHORT STORIES, FABLES, AND LESSER-KNOWN WRITINGS, REVISED EDITION by Anne Frank, edited by Gerrold Van Der Stroom and Susan Massotty, translated by Susan Massotty, copyright © 1982 and 2003 by Anne Frank-Fonds, Basel, for all texts of Anne Frank. English translation copyright © 2003 by Susan Massotty; used by permission of Doubleday, an imprint of the Knopf Doubleday Publishing Group, a division of Penguin Random House LLC. All rights reserved. **Ross Gay:** "A Small Needful Fact" first appeared in SPLIT

THIS ROCK (www.splitthisrock.org). Reprinted by permission of the author. **X González:** Extract previously published by HarpersBazaar.com, "Parkland Student X González Opens Up About Their Fight for Gun Control," February 2018. Written by X González. Reprinted by permission of Hearst Magazine Media, Inc and JONESWORKS on behalf of X González. **Frances Hardinge:** (UK) Extract from DEEPLIGHT, first published in 2019 by Macmillan Children's Books, an imprint of Pan Macmillan, copyright © Frances Hardinge 2019; extract from THE LIE TREE first published in 2013 by Pan Macmillan, a division of Macmillan Publishers International Limited, copyright © Frances Hardinge 2013; reproduced by permission of Macmillan Publishers International Limited. (US & Canada) Extract from DEEPLIGHT by Frances Hardinge, text copyright 2019 © by Frances Hardinge; extract from THE LIE TREE by Frances Hardinge, text copyright © 2016 by Frances Hardinge; used by permission of Amulet Books, an imprint of ABRAMS, New York. All rights reserved. **Stephen Hawking:** Extract from Professor Hawking's interview with ABC's Diane Sawyer in June 2010, reprinted by permission of United Agents on behalf of the Estate of Stephen Hawking. **Langston Hughes:** (World ebook & UK print) "April Rain Song" from THE COLLECTED POEMS OF LANGSTON HUGHES, Alfred A Knopf Inc, reprinted by permission of David Higham Associates. (US & Canada print) "April Rain Song" from THE COLLECTED POEMS OF LANGSTON HUGHES by Langston Hughes, edited by Arnold Rampersad with David Roessel, Associate Editor, copyright © 1994 by the Estate of Langston Hughes. Used by permission of Alfred A. Knopf, an imprint of the Knopf Doubleday Publishing Group, a division of Penguin Random House LLC. All rights reserved. **Eva Ibbotson:** (UK & Canada) Extracts from JOURNEY TO THE RIVER SEA, first published in 2001 by Macmillan Children's Books, an imprint of Pan Macmillan, a division of Macmillan Publishers International Limited. Reproduced by permission of Macmillan Publishers International Limited. Copyright © Eva Ibbotson 2001. (US) Excerpts from JOURNEY TO THE RIVER SEA by Eva Ibbotson, copyright © 2001 by Eva Ibbotson. Used by permission of Dutton Children's Books, an imprint of Penguin Young Readers Group, a division of Penguin Random House LLC. All rights reserved. **Tove Jansson:** Extract from MOOMINVALLEY IN NOVEMBER © Tove Jansson (1970), Moomin Characters™, reprinted by permission of R & B Licensing AB on behalf of Oy Moomin Characters Ltd. **Oliver Jeffers:** Extract from HERE WE ARE: NOTES FOR LIVING ON PLANET EARTH, reprinted by permission of HarperCollins Publishers Ltd, © Oliver Jeffers 2017. **Steve Jobs:** Extract from Steve Jobs' 2005

Stanford commencement address, reprinted by permission of Apple Inc. and the Estate of Steve Jobs. **Katherine Johnson:** Quotation by Katherine Johnson from "Katherine Johnson: A Lifetime of STEM" www.nasa.gov/audienceforeducators/ a-lifetime-of-stem.html. **Dr Martin Luther King, Jr.:** Extract from Dr. Martin Luther King, Jr.'s "I have a dream" speech, reprinted by arrangement with The Heirs to the Estate of Martin Luther King Jr., c/o Writers House as agent for the proprietor New York, NY. Copyright © 1963 by Dr. Martin Luther King, Jr. Renewed © 1991 by Coretta Scott King. **Ursula K. Le Guin:** Extract copyright © 2003 by Ursula K. Le Guin. First appeared in THE LANGUAGE OF THE NIGHT, published by G.P. Putnam & Sons in 1979. Reprinted by permission of Curtis Brown, Ltd. **C.S. Lewis:** Extracts from THE LION, THE WITCH AND THE WARDROBE by C.S. Lewis © copyright CS Lewis Pte Ltd 1950, and THE VOYAGE OF THE DAWN TREADER by C.S. Lewis © copyright CS Lewis Pte Ltd 1952, reprinted by permission of the CS Lewis Company Ltd. **George R.R. Martin:** Extract from A DANCE WITH DRAGONS, reprinted by permission of HarperCollins Publishers Ltd, © George R. R. Martin 2011. **Robert R. McCammon:** (World ebook & UK print) Extract from BOY'S LIFE by Robert R. McCammon. Copyright © 1991 by the McCammon Corporation. All rights reserved. Reprinted by permission of the Donald Maass Literary Agency on behalf of the McCammon Corporation. (US & Canada print) Extract from BOY'S LIFE by Robert R. McCammon. Copyright © 1991 by the McCammon Corporation. Reprinted with the permission of Atria Books, a division of Simon & Schuster, Inc. All rights reserved. **Roger McGough:** "The Leader" from SKY IN THE PIE by Roger McGough, reprinted by permission of Peters Fraser & Dunlop (www.petersfraserdunlop.com) on behalf of Roger McGough. **Hilary McKay:** "War and the Simpsons" from LINES IN THE SAND: NEW WRITING ON WAR AND PEACE, edited by Mary Hoffman and Rhiannon Lassiter, Frances Lincoln 2003, copyright © 2003 by Hilary McKay, reprinted by permission of The Bent Agency UK Ltd on behalf of Hilary McKay. **Peter Medawar:** Extract from Peter Medawar's Presidential Address to the British Association for the Advancement of Science, Exeter, 3 September 1969. **Harvey Milk:** Quotation from Harvey Milk, reproduced by permission of the Harvey Milk Foundation. For more information please visit www.milkfoundation.org. **A.A. Milne:** (UK print) Extract from THE HOUSE AT POOH CORNER by A.A. Milne. Text copyright © The Trustees of the Pooh Properties 1928. Published by Egmont UK Ltd and used with permission. (US & Canada print) Excerpt from THE HOUSE AT POOH CORNER by A.A. Milne, copyright 1928 by Penguin Random House LLC. Copyright © renewed 1956 by A.A. Milne. Used by permission of Dutton Children's Books, an imprint of Penguin Young Readers Group, a division of Penguin Random House LLC. All rights reserved. (World ebook) Text by A.A. Milne copyright © The Trustees of the Pooh Properties 1928. Reproduced with permissions from Curtis Brown Group Limited on behalf of The Trustees of the Pooh Properties. **Tim Minchin:** Naughty (from "Matilda The Musical"). Words & Music by Tim Minchin. © Copyright 2011 Navel Enterprises Pty Ltd. Print rights exclusively administered by Hal Leonard Europe Limited. All Rights Reserved. International Copyright Secured. Used by permission of Hal Leonard Europe Limited. **Lin-Manuel Miranda:** "THE ROOM WHERE IT HAPPENS" and "WAIT FOR IT" © 2015 5000 Broadway Music (ASCAP). All rights administered by WC Music Corp. **Barack Obama:** Extract from Barack Obama's campaign speech, 5 February 2008 www.nytimes. com/2008/02/05/us/politics/05text-obama.html. **R. J. Palacio:** (UK) Extract from WONDER by R. J. Palacio. Published by Corgi Children. Reprinted by permission of The Random House Group Limited. © 2014. (US & Canada) Excerpt from WONDER by R. J. Palacio, copyright © 2012 by R. J. Palacio. Used by permission of Alfred A. Knopf, an imprint of Random House Children's Books, a division of Penguin Random House LLC. All rights reserved. **Rosa Parks:** (World print) Excerpt from ROSA PARKS: MY STORY by Rosa Parks with Jim Haskins, copyright © 1992 by Rosa Parks. Used by permission of Dial Books for Young Readers, an imprint of Penguin Young Readers Group, a division of Penguin Random House LLC. All rights reserved. (World ebook) Extract from ROSA PARKS: MY STORY by Rosa Parks with Jim Haskins, Dial Books for Young Readers 1992, copyright © 1992 by Rosa Parks, used by permission of The Betsy Nolan Literary Agency. **Justin Paul & Benj Pasek:** You Will Be Found. Words & Music by Justin Paul & Benj Pasek. © Copyright 2017 Breathelike Music/Pick In A Pinch Music. Kobalt Music Publishing Limited. All Rights Reserved. International Copyright Secured. Used by permission of Hal Leonard Europe Limited. **Philip Pullman:** (UK) Extract from CLOCKWORK by Philip Pullman. Copyright © Philip Pullman, 1996. Reprinted by permission of Penguin Books Ltd. Extracts from THE AMBER SPYGLASS. Copyright © Philip Pullman, 2000. Reproduced with the permission of Scholastic Ltd. All Rights Reserved. (US & Canada) Extract from CLOCKWORK, copyright © Philip Pullman, reprinted by permission of Scholastic Inc. Excerpts from HIS DARK MATERIALS: THE AMBER SPYGLASS (BOOK 3) by Philip Pullman, copyright © 2000 by Philip Pullman. Used by permission of Alfred A. Knopf, an imprint of Random House

Children's Books, a division of Penguin Random House LLC. All rights reserved. **Michael Rosen:** Text © 2004 Michael Rosen. MICHAEL ROSEN'S SAD BOOK by Michael Rosen & illustrated by Quentin Blake. Reproduced by permission of Walker Books Ltd, London SE11 5HJ, www.walker.co.uk. **Katherine Rundell:** The Agreed Upon 17 Words by Katherine Rundell. Published by Simon & Schuster. Copyright © Katherine Rundell. Reproduced by permission of the author c/o Rogers, Coleridge & White Ltd., 20 Powis Mews, London W11 1JN. (UK & Canada) Extracts from ROOFTOPPERS by Katherine Rundell, copyright © Katherine Rundell 2013, reprinted by permission of Faber and Faber Ltd. (US) Extracts from ROOFTOPPERS by Katherine Rundell. Text copyright © 2013 by Katherine Rundell. Reprinted with the permission of Simon & Schuster Books for Young Readers, an imprint of Simon & Schuster Children's Publishing Division. All rights reserved. **Bertrand Russell:** Extract from Bertrand Russell's 1959 BBC interview, reprinted with permission of the BBC and the Bertrand Russell Peace Foundation Ltd. **Dr. Seuss:** (UK) Extract from I CAN READ WITH MY EYES SHUT by Dr. Seuss. Reprinted by permission of HarperCollins Publishers Ltd. © 1978 by Dr. Seuss Enterprises, L.P. Extract from YERTLE THE TURTLE AND OTHER STORIES by Dr. Seuss. Copyright © by Dr. Seuss Enterprises, L.P. 1950, 1951, 1958, renewed 1977, 1979, 1986. Reprinted by permission of Dr. Seuss Enterprises, L.P. (US & Canada) Excerpt from I CAN READ WITH MY EYES SHUT by Dr. Seuss, TM and copyright © 1978 by Dr. Seuss Enterprises, L.P.; excerpt from YERTLE THE TURTLE AND OTHER STORIES by Dr. Seuss, TM & copyright © by Dr. Seuss Enterprises, L.P. 1950, 1951, 1958; used by permission of Random House Children's Books, a division of Penguin Random House LLC. All rights reserved. **Dodie Smith:** (UK) Extract from I CAPTURE THE CASTLE by Dodie Smith. Published by Vintage Classics. Reprinted by permission of The Random House Group Limited. © 2004. (US & Canada) Extract from I CAPTURE THE CASTLE © 1998 by Dodie Smith. Reprinted by permission of St. Martin's Press. All Rights Reserved. **Stephen Sondheim:** Children Will Listen (from "Into The Woods"). Words & Music by Stephen Sondheim. © Copyright 1987 Rilting Music Incorporated. Print Rights administered by Hal Leonard Europe Limited. All Rights Reserved. International Copyright Secured. Used by permission of Hal Leonard Europe Limited. **Robin Stevens:** (UK) Twenty-six (26) words from TOP MARKS FOR MURDER by Robin Stevens (Puffin Books, 2019). Copyright © Robin Stevens 2019. Reprinted by permission of Penguin Books Ltd. (US & Canada) Extract from TOP MARKS FOR MURDER by Robin Stevens, Puffin Books 2019, copyright © Robin Stevens 2019, reprinted by permission of The

Bent Agency UK Ltd. **Dylan Thomas:** (UK) Extract from A CHILD'S CHRISTMAS IN WALES, Orion Children's Books, copyright © The Dylan Thomas Trust, reprinted by permission of David Higham Associates. (US & Canada) Extract by Dylan Thomas, from A CHILD'S CHRISTMAS IN WALES, copyright © 1954 by New Directions Publishing Corp. Reprinted by permission of New Directions Publishing Corp. **Greta Thunberg:** Extract from Greta Thunberg's Extinction Rebellion Speech Outside Parliament Square www.facebook.com/ExtinctionRebellion/videos/greta-thunberg-full-speech-at-parliament-square/2215034952158269 (2019). **Kurt Vonnegut:** Extract from GOD BLESS YOU, MR ROSEWATER, first published in Great Britain by Jonathan Cape in 1965, copyright © Kurt Vonnegut Jr 1965. **Malala Yousafzai:** Reproduced with permission of Curtis Brown Group Ltd, on behalf of Malala Yousafzai Copyright © Malala Yousafzai, 2013 Malala Yousafzai's Speech to the United Nations. **Benjamin Zephaniah:** 27 (twenty-seven) lines and 177 (one hundred and seventy-seven) words from "THE BRITISH" from WICKED WORLD! by Benjamin Zephaniah (Penguin Books 2000). Copyright © Benjamin Zephaniah, 2000; 7 (seven) lines and 27 (twenty-seven) words from "WHO'S WHO" from TALKING TURKEYS by Benjamin Zephaniah (Penguin Books 1995). Copyright © Benjamin Zephaniah, 1995; reprinted by permission of Penguin Books Ltd.

Every effort has been made to obtain permission to reproduce copyright material, but there may have been cases where we have been unable to trace a copyright holder. The publisher would be happy to correct any omissions in future printings.

ABOUT THE AUTHOR

Nicolette Jones has spent a lot of her life reading, for work and for fun (mostly both at once). She has written about children's books for *The Sunday Times* for decades, has judged quite a few book prizes, chaired bookish events at festivals, read aloud a great deal to her children, taught writing, and written books of her own for both adults and young people. Her head is full of characters and stories and poetry and bits of writing she remembers and savours. She cannot promise always to have followed all the good advice in the pieces chosen here, so she will entirely understand if you don't always either.